Russ Cook

A Run Like No Other

John Lucas Whitehead

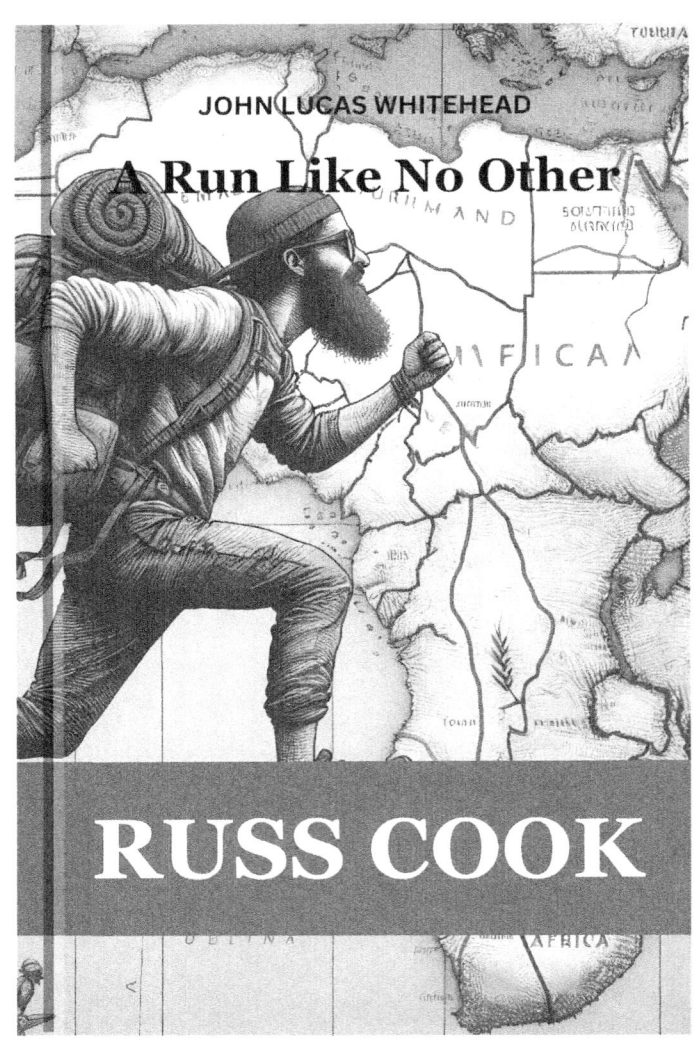

Copyright © 2024 by John Lucas Whitehead

All rights reserved. No part of this publication may be reproduced, distributed, or transmitted in any form or by any means, including photocopying, recording, or other electronic or mechanical methods, without the prior written permission of the publisher, except in the case of brief quotations embodied in critical reviews and certain other noncommercial uses permitted by copyright law.

Table of Contents

Chapter 1: The Man Behind "The Hardest Geezer" 7
- Early Life and Struggles 7
- Overcoming Mental Health, Gambling, and Drinking 9
- Motivation to Make a Difference 12

Chapter 2: Preparing for the Challenge 19
- Concept and Planning: Running the Length of Africa 19
- Training and Physical Preparation 25
- Setting Off: Cape Agulhas, South Africa 32

Chapter 3: Facing the Continent's Challenges 37
- Navigating Africa: Countries, Cities, and Landscapes 37
- Visa Complications and Geopolitical Hurdles. 43
- Dealing with Health Scares and Injury 49

Chapter 4: Setbacks and Survival 55
- The Armed Robbery in Angola 55
- Going Missing in the Congo Jungle 60
- Coping with Dehydration, Food Poisoning, and Back Pain 64

Chapter 5: Pushing Through Adversity 69
- The Power of Mental Fortitude 69
- Securing the Algerian Visa with Public Support.. 73
- Surviving the Sahara: Sandstorms and Night Runs 76

Chapter 6: Completing the Mission 81
- The Final Push: Running Through Tunisia 81
- Reaching Ras Ben Sakka: The Finish Line 84

Celebrations, Supporters, and Reflections..... 88
**Chapter 7: What's Next for the Hardest Geezer?.
93**
    Teasing Future Challenges: Pole to Pole........ 93
    The Impact of the Africa Run: Fundraising and Awareness.. 96

Chapter 1: The Man Behind "The Hardest Geezer"

Early Life and Struggles

Russ Cook, now famously known as the "Hardest Geezer," had a humble upbringing in Worthing, West Sussex, a seaside town on England's southern coast. Growing up, Cook led what might be considered a typical British life, but beneath the surface, he faced personal struggles that would later shape the tenacity and resilience for which he's now celebrated.

As a young man, Cook battled with issues common to many, such as mental health challenges, struggles with self-discipline, and a period where he found himself lost in negative cycles of gambling and drinking. These behaviors were rooted in the pressures and anxieties that many young people face, but for Cook, they became defining elements of his early life. He often speaks candidly about this difficult period, acknowledging how these struggles helped him gain perspective and the hunger to push himself beyond his limits.

While he wasn't an athlete in his formative years, Cook's passion for adventure and pushing boundaries was always simmering beneath the surface. His early twenties saw him turn a corner.

Realizing the destructive path he was on, he decided to channel his energy into something more positive and productive. This marked a pivotal change in his life.

He found running to be an outlet—a way to escape from his past mistakes and mental challenges. What started as a form of release gradually evolved into a means to test his physical and mental endurance. The transition wasn't easy, but each run, no matter how small, represented progress. With no formal athletic background, Cook demonstrated that personal transformation doesn't come from perfection, but from persistence.

Russ Cook's early life is a testament to the power of self-awareness and the desire for change. His struggles didn't define him; they motivated him. Instead of allowing his personal challenges to dictate his future, Cook used them as fuel to embark on some of the world's most extreme endurance challenges, including running the length of Africa. The lessons he learned in those early years became the foundation for his remarkable mindset—the very mindset that has led him to become one of the most inspiring ultrarunners of his generation.

Overcoming Mental Health, Gambling, and Drinking

Russ Cook's journey to becoming an ultrarunner and endurance athlete wasn't just a physical challenge—it was also an immense mental battle. Before becoming the "Hardest Geezer," Cook struggled with personal demons, including mental health issues, gambling, and drinking, which threatened to derail his life.

Mental Health Struggles
In his early twenties, Cook found himself grappling with the pressures and uncertainties of life, leading to bouts of anxiety and low self-esteem. Like many young adults, he struggled to find his purpose and direction, which left him feeling unfulfilled and overwhelmed. Instead of confronting these feelings head-on, Cook found temporary escapes in unhealthy habits that only compounded his problems.

During this period, he felt trapped, unable to envision a future where things could be different. His mental health took a toll on his motivation, and he became stuck in a cycle of negative self-talk and frustration. It was an internal struggle that many can relate to, where the weight of everyday pressures clouded his sense of purpose. But Cook was determined to find a way out and sought an outlet to break free from this cycle of despair.

Struggles with Gambling

One of the most dangerous habits Cook fell into was gambling. What began as a casual pastime escalated into an addiction that consumed not only his time but also his finances. Like many others who suffer from gambling addiction, Cook found himself chasing losses, convinced that one big win could solve his problems. Instead, this habit deepened his sense of failure, creating financial strain and increasing his stress levels.

Cook has since spoken openly about how destructive his gambling behavior became. It left him feeling isolated and further distanced from the life he wanted to lead. He recognized that his gambling was not just about money—it was about filling a void and escaping from the emotional pain and dissatisfaction that plagued him.

Drinking as an Escape

Alongside gambling, Cook turned to alcohol as a way to numb his feelings and escape from reality. What started as social drinking quickly spiraled into something more harmful. Drinking became a way for him to avoid facing his struggles, but it only deepened his sense of helplessness. The temporary relief alcohol provided was quickly replaced by regret and self-doubt.

Cook's unhealthy relationship with drinking perpetuated a cycle of poor decision-making and self-sabotage. Rather than dealing with the underlying issues, he masked them, pushing his problems further down the road. But he soon realized that he was only digging himself deeper into a hole from which he needed to escape.

Turning Point

The turning point in Cook's life came when he recognized that these destructive habits were leading him nowhere. His mind and body were suffering, and he knew he needed to make a change. He decided to quit gambling and drinking, acknowledging that they were not solutions to his problems but rather the very things keeping him from living the life he wanted.

Determined to reclaim control, Cook made a conscious decision to focus on something more constructive. He turned to running as a way to cope with his mental health and to find clarity. Running provided him with a sense of freedom and control—things that he had lost during his struggles. Each mile became a victory, a step toward reclaiming his life.

Running gave him the mental and emotional release he needed, and over time, it became his therapy. With each run, he distanced himself further from the habits that had once held him back. Instead of escaping from his problems, he learned to confront them through physical challenge and self-discipline.

Cook's journey to overcoming his struggles with mental health, gambling, and drinking is a story of resilience. He used running not just to heal physically but also mentally, proving that no matter how far someone falls, there is always a way to rise again. Today, he uses his platform to inspire others to face their challenges head-on and to seek healthier ways of coping with life's difficulties. His story stands as a powerful reminder that recovery is possible and that personal transformation is within reach for anyone willing to fight for it.

Motivation to Make a Difference

Russ Cook, famously known as the "Hardest Geezer," is much more than an ultramarathon runner and endurance athlete. Behind his extreme physical feats lies a deep, driving purpose—to make a real difference in the world. His motivation extends far beyond setting records or personal achievement; it is rooted in a desire to inspire change, raise awareness, and support charitable causes that address important social issues.

From battling his own mental health struggles to recognizing the power of perseverance, Cook's story is one of personal transformation and social responsibility. His experiences have shaped his commitment to helping others and contributing to society in meaningful ways. Below are the key factors that drive Cook's motivation to make a difference.

Personal Transformation and Mental Health Awareness
One of the most significant motivations for Cook's challenges comes from his own battle with mental health issues. Having struggled with anxiety,

gambling, and drinking, Cook's life could have easily taken a different turn. He has been candid about the internal battles that once held him back and how they shaped his outlook on life.

Running became his escape from those destructive patterns and ultimately a tool for self-improvement. Each grueling run allowed Cook to confront his mental and emotional pain, providing him with a sense of control and purpose. As he began to conquer personal challenges through physical endurance, he realized the mental health benefits that came with it. This personal discovery became a key motivator for Cook to raise awareness about mental health and inspire others who might be struggling in silence.

Cook uses his platform to encourage conversations around mental health, particularly among young people. He knows from experience how isolating and overwhelming mental health struggles can be, and his willingness to be vulnerable about his own experiences has made him a relatable figure. By showcasing his own recovery through endurance challenges, Cook hopes to inspire others to seek healthier outlets for their emotions and challenges, reinforcing the idea that anyone can overcome obstacles with the right mindset and support.

Charity and Giving Back to the Community

Cook's motivation to make a difference goes beyond personal transformation. A key aspect of his endurance challenges is his dedication to raising funds and awareness for charitable causes. During his Africa run, Cook raised significant amounts of money for two specific charities: The Running Charity and Sandblast Ltd.

- The Running Charity: This organization uses running and fitness to empower young people who are experiencing homelessness or dealing with complex needs. Cook resonated deeply with the charity's mission because he understands how powerful physical activity can be in helping individuals cope with life's difficulties. He believes that running and fitness offer a sense of freedom, discipline, and achievement, which can be transformative for individuals who are struggling. By partnering with The Running Charity, Cook seeks to help at-risk youth regain confidence, develop resilience, and find a path toward personal growth and stability.

- Sandblast Ltd: Sandblast is an organization dedicated to raising awareness of Sahrawi culture and supporting the Sahrawi people, who have been displaced due to territorial disputes in the Western Sahara. Cook's commitment to this cause highlights his broader concern for global social justice issues. Through his African journey, Cook had the opportunity to witness the beauty and struggles of different cultures across the continent. His collaboration with Sandblast is a reflection of his desire to give a voice to marginalized communities and educate the world about their struggles.

Through his charitable efforts, Cook has raised hundreds of thousands of pounds to support these causes. His motivation stems from a desire to give back to the communities and people he encounters during his runs, using his physical challenges as a means to inspire generosity and compassion in others.

Inspiring Others to Push Boundaries

Cook's motivation to make a difference also lies in his desire to inspire others to challenge their own limits—both physically and mentally. Through his ultramarathon runs, Cook has demonstrated the human capacity for endurance, resilience, and overcoming adversity. His motto is simple: If he can do it, anyone can.

Cook's challenges are not just about personal glory or breaking records—they are about proving what is possible. Whether it's running 71 marathons in 66 days from Asia to England or completing over 10,000 miles across the length of Africa, Cook's extreme feats serve as a metaphor for life. He often speaks about how every marathon is a reflection of life's challenges: they require determination, persistence, and a willingness to keep moving forward even when the road seems impossible.

By documenting his experiences and sharing them through social media platforms like Instagram, YouTube, and X (formerly Twitter), Cook hopes to inspire people from all walks of life to push their boundaries. Whether someone is struggling with self-doubt, facing personal challenges, or simply looking for motivation, Cook's story serves as a powerful reminder that human potential is limitless.

Cook frequently interacts with his followers, encouraging them to take up their own personal challenges—no matter how big or small. His motivation comes from the idea that everyone has untapped potential and the ability to overcome their own struggles, and he aims to create a ripple effect of positive change by sharing his story.

Adventure, Discovery, and Connecting with the World

Beyond the physical challenge, part of Cook's motivation lies in his sense of adventure and his desire to discover more about the world and its people. His runs take him through a diverse range of landscapes, cultures, and communities, and each journey is an opportunity to learn and grow.

During his run across Africa, Cook experienced everything from the scorching heat of the Namib Desert to the dense jungles of the Congo. He encountered kindness from strangers, built relationships with locals, and learned about different ways of life. For Cook, these experiences are deeply meaningful. They remind him of the interconnectedness of humanity and the importance of empathy and understanding.

By running through some of the most remote and challenging regions of the world, Cook hopes to shine a light on the beauty and complexity of the places he visits. His motivation is not just to complete the challenge but to build connections along the way, fostering a deeper appreciation for the diversity of human experience. In his own words, he often reflects on how the kindness of others has been one of the most rewarding parts of his journey.

Leaving a Legacy of Courage and Compassion
Ultimately, Russ Cook's motivation is about leaving a lasting legacy. He wants his story to serve as a testament to the power of perseverance, courage, and compassion. His physical endurance may be impressive, but it is his dedication to making the world a better place that defines his legacy. Cook hopes that by raising awareness for important causes, inspiring others to push their limits, and highlighting the resilience of the human spirit, he can leave behind a legacy that will continue to make a difference long after his challenges are over.

Through his fundraising efforts, mental health advocacy, and personal interactions with people from around the world, Cook is driven by a deep desire to create positive change. His motivation is not just about personal achievement, but about encouraging others to believe in their own capacity to make a difference, no matter the obstacles they face.

In every step of his journey, Cook is motivated by the idea that we all have the power to leave the world a better place than we found it—whether through charity, compassion, or simply inspiring others to believe in themselves.

Chapter 2: Preparing for the Challenge

Concept and Planning: Running the Length of Africa

Russ Cook's decision to run the entire length of Africa from the southernmost tip to the northernmost point was nothing short of audacious. The concept of this challenge was both physically and logistically complex, requiring meticulous planning, intense preparation, and an unbreakable mindset to tackle the unpredictability of such a massive undertaking. Cook's ambition was not just about achieving a personal milestone; it was about pushing the boundaries of human endurance and inspiring others through the sheer magnitude of the challenge. The journey spanned almost a year, with over 10,000 miles of running across diverse terrains, climates, and cultural landscapes, with each step serving a larger purpose.

Conceptualizing the Challenge
The idea of running the length of Africa was born out of Cook's desire to achieve something that had never been done before. He had previously completed significant endurance challenges, such as running 71 marathons in 66 days from Istanbul to London in 2019. While those challenges were remarkable in their own right, Cook felt that he

needed to take on something even more daunting, something that would truly test the limits of his mental and physical resilience.

The idea of running across Africa stood out as a monumental feat that few, if any, had ever completed in the way Cook envisioned. The African continent, with its vast array of landscapes—from deserts to rainforests—posed a unique set of challenges that would require not only physical strength but also mental fortitude. Cook believed that running the length of Africa would serve as the ultimate endurance test, not just for the sheer distance but for the unpredictability of the journey itself.

In addition to the personal challenge, Cook's motivation for this run was deeply tied to raising awareness for mental health issues and raising funds for charitable causes. By taking on an endeavor that seemed almost impossible, Cook hoped to demonstrate to others that even the biggest challenges can be overcome with determination, discipline, and purpose.

The Route and Logistical Considerations

Planning the route was one of the most critical aspects of the entire challenge. Africa is the second-largest continent in the world, and its diverse geography, political borders, and unpredictable weather patterns made Cook's journey incredibly complex. The initial goal was to cover approximately 9,320 miles (15,000 km), but due to various complications, the final distance extended beyond 10,190 miles (16,400 km).

The route Cook chose began at Cape Agulhas, the southernmost point of Africa in South Africa, and concluded at Ras Ben Sakka in Tunisia, the northernmost point of the continent. His journey took him through 16 countries, including South Africa, Namibia, Angola, Democratic Republic of Congo, Cameroon, Nigeria, Benin, Togo, Ivory Coast, Guinea, Senegal, Mauritania, and Algeria, among others. Each of these countries presented its own set of logistical challenges, from securing visas to navigating remote and often dangerous territories.

One of the primary challenges Cook faced in the planning stages was ensuring he had the proper support and infrastructure to sustain himself during the run. Given the extreme environments he would encounter—such as the Namib Desert, the Congo Rainforest, and the vast Sahara Desert—adequate preparation for hydration, food, and rest was crucial. Cook and his team meticulously planned the logistics of providing food and water in areas where resources were scarce, as well as preparing for potential medical emergencies. They also had to plan for accommodation, transportation for the support team, and the constant management of visas and border crossings.

Another crucial consideration was security. Some regions of Africa are known for political instability, and Cook had to factor in the potential risks of running through these areas. This required careful planning with local authorities and communities to ensure his safety. For instance, Cook and his team experienced an armed robbery in Angola, where they had cameras, cash, and passports stolen, highlighting the unpredictable nature of the challenge.

Preparing Physically and Mentally
The physical demands of running over 10,000 miles required Cook to be in peak condition. However, his preparation went beyond simply logging miles in training. Endurance running at such an extreme level requires an intricate understanding of how the body reacts to long periods of exertion, as well as the mental strength to push through pain, fatigue, and adversity.

To prepare, Cook undertook an intense training regimen focused on building endurance, strength, and resilience. This included running long distances every day, often through difficult terrain to mimic the environments he would face in Africa. He also incorporated cross-training exercises such as strength workouts, yoga, and flexibility exercises to improve his physical resilience and minimize the risk of injury.

Nutrition played a crucial role in his preparation. Cook needed to fuel his body with the right balance of carbohydrates, proteins, and fats to sustain energy levels during long runs. His diet was tailored to maximize endurance while ensuring he had enough reserves to handle extreme conditions. Hydration was also a critical aspect of his preparation, particularly in anticipation of running through deserts where water would be limited.

Beyond physical preparation, Cook knew that the mental demands of running the length of Africa would be even more challenging. The psychological toll of running day after day, often in isolation and under extreme conditions, required immense mental strength. Cook prepared mentally by focusing on mindfulness techniques and visualization exercises to help him stay present and overcome the inevitable moments of doubt. He understood that mental resilience would be the key to enduring the pain, exhaustion, and emotional highs and lows that would accompany such a long and grueling challenge.

Cook also prepared for the emotional and psychological impact of being away from home and his support network for such an extended period. The isolation of running through remote regions with little contact with family and friends meant that he needed to rely on his inner strength and the support of his team to keep him going.

Building a Support Team

No endurance challenge of this magnitude could be completed without a dedicated support team. Cook's team played an essential role in ensuring that he had everything he needed to succeed, from logistical coordination to providing emotional support when the going got tough.

The team was responsible for managing the day-to-day logistics of the run, including securing accommodations, planning rest stops, and coordinating with local authorities for border crossings and security. They also handled medical needs, ensuring Cook received proper care when he experienced injuries or illnesses during the run.

In addition, the team helped Cook document his journey and share it with the world. Throughout the challenge, Cook shared updates on social media platforms like Instagram, YouTube, and X (formerly Twitter), where he documented the highs and lows of the journey. The support team was instrumental in managing these accounts, helping Cook maintain a connection with his followers and raising awareness for the charities he was supporting.

Final Preparations and Setting Off

After months of planning, training, and logistical coordination, Cook was finally ready to begin his challenge. On April 22, 2023, he set off from Cape Agulhas in South Africa, starting his 352-day journey to run the length of the African continent. The enormity of the challenge was evident from the very beginning—Cook would need to run an average of more than 29 miles (46 km) per day, all while contending with physical fatigue, unpredictable weather, and logistical complications.

Cook's mental and emotional focus at the start of the journey was clear. In one of his early Instagram posts, he reflected on the challenge ahead, saying, "Tougher days are yet to come of course, and they will be the toughest I've ever faced, no doubt. I'm ready to attack them all." These words encapsulated the mindset that would carry him through the next 12 months—the determination to face every obstacle head-on and push through even the most difficult moments.

The early stages of the run were marked by excitement and anticipation, but as Cook progressed further into the journey, the true scale of the challenge became apparent. The planning, preparation, and support that had gone into the run proved invaluable, but the real test would be how Cook and his team responded to the countless challenges that lay ahead.

Training and Physical Preparation

Russ Cook's decision to run the entire length of Africa required not just an indomitable spirit, but also an extreme level of physical preparedness. Running over 10,000 miles across diverse and often harsh terrains demands more than the average endurance training. Cook knew that his body would need to be conditioned not just for the rigors of daily long-distance running but also for the unpredictable challenges of varying climates, altitudes, and surfaces. His training and physical preparation were crucial for success and involved a comprehensive approach that included endurance building, injury prevention, strength training, and recovery.

1. Building Endurance for Ultramarathon Running
Endurance was the cornerstone of Russ Cook's training regimen. To prepare for an expedition that would require him to run an average of 29 miles (46 km) per day for almost a year, Cook needed to gradually build up his body's capacity for sustained long-distance running.

Long-Distance Runs:
Cook began by incorporating progressively longer runs into his routine, mimicking the distances he would need to cover daily in Africa. Over time, he increased the intensity and distance of these runs, often pushing himself to exceed marathon distances multiple times a week. This helped his body adapt to the constant strain that daily running would entail.

Back-to-Back Runs:
Cook's body needed to recover quickly between runs, as the challenge required daily effort with little rest. To simulate this, he trained with "back-to-back" long runs, running significant distances on consecutive days to build resilience and ensure his muscles could recover and perform consistently. This technique helped Cook prepare for the physical reality of being on his feet every day for almost a year without the luxury of taking prolonged recovery breaks.

Terrain-Specific Training:
Given the variety of terrains Cook would encounter—deserts, rainforests, savannahs, jungles, and cities—he designed his training to

reflect these diverse conditions. He incorporated runs through sand, gravel, forests, and hills to condition his legs to handle the uneven, unpredictable surfaces that he would face in places like the Namib Desert and the Congo Rainforest. The varied terrain helped to strengthen different muscle groups and improve his overall agility and balance, reducing the likelihood of injury in unfamiliar environments.

2. Injury Prevention and Strength Training
For an undertaking of this magnitude, injury prevention was paramount. Even a minor injury could derail the challenge, so Cook's training placed a heavy emphasis on building strength and resilience to prevent breakdowns over time.
Core Strength and Stability:
Cook recognized that running long distances, especially over uneven surfaces, puts a significant strain on the body's core. To build a solid foundation, he incorporated a variety of core-strengthening exercises into his routine, such as planks, crunches, and stability exercises. A strong core helps maintain proper posture and running form, which can reduce the risk of injury, especially when fatigue sets in during long runs.
Leg and Lower Body Strength:
Since his legs would bear the brunt of the effort, Cook also focused on building strength in his quadriceps, hamstrings, calves, and glutes. He used weight training, squats, lunges, and hill sprints to develop muscle power and endurance in his

lower body. This not only improved his running efficiency but also helped him tackle the uphill and downhill segments of his run across Africa.

Flexibility and Mobility:

Cook also incorporated stretching, yoga, and mobility drills into his regimen to ensure his muscles remained flexible and supple. Tight muscles are prone to strains and tears, so flexibility was essential to keeping his body in top condition. Regular stretching sessions also aided in his recovery, reducing soreness after long runs and allowing his muscles to remain limber despite the daily strain.

Cross-Training:

To avoid overuse injuries that can result from repetitive running, Cook engaged in cross-training activities such as swimming and cycling. These low-impact exercises allowed him to maintain his cardiovascular fitness while giving his joints and muscles a break from the constant pounding they would endure while running. Cross-training also helped to balance out muscle imbalances that might develop from repetitive running motions.

3. Nutrition and Hydration

Fueling his body correctly was critical to maintaining energy levels during his extensive training sessions. Cook's diet was tailored to provide the necessary energy, muscle recovery, and hydration required for endurance athletes.

Carbohydrates for Energy:

As an endurance athlete, Cook's body needed a constant supply of carbohydrates to fuel his long-distance runs. He consumed a high-carbohydrate diet that included whole grains, vegetables, fruits, and legumes. Carbohydrates are essential for maintaining glycogen stores, which are the primary energy source during prolonged physical activity.

Protein for Recovery:
Protein was also a critical component of Cook's diet, as it helps repair and rebuild muscle tissue that breaks down during intense training. He focused on lean protein sources such as chicken, fish, eggs, and plant-based options to aid in muscle recovery and promote healing. Given the toll that daily running would take on his body, maintaining a sufficient intake of protein was crucial for long-term endurance.

Hydration and Electrolyte Balance:
Running through deserts and other hot climates meant that dehydration would be a constant risk. To prepare for this, Cook trained with a focus on hydration, ensuring he replenished lost fluids and electrolytes. He regularly consumed water and electrolyte-rich drinks, particularly during long training sessions where he would lose significant amounts of sweat. In preparation for the extreme heat he would face in the Sahara Desert, Cook trained in hot conditions, conditioning his body to retain hydration and perform efficiently in those environments.

4. Mental Preparation and Building Toughness
Physical preparation alone would not be enough to complete the challenge. Cook needed to develop the mental resilience to push through the pain, exhaustion, and inevitable setbacks he would face during his year-long run.

Mindfulness and Meditation:
Cook incorporated mindfulness techniques to stay present and maintain focus during long runs. He used meditation to calm his mind, especially when fatigue or doubt began to creep in. By learning to stay focused on each step, rather than the overwhelming distance ahead, Cook was able to break down the challenge into manageable segments.

Visualizing Success:
One of Cook's most important mental strategies was visualization. Before beginning his run, he spent time imagining the challenges he would face and mentally rehearsing how he would overcome them. Whether it was visualizing the finish line at Tunisia or picturing himself running through difficult terrain, this mental rehearsal helped build confidence and prepared him for the inevitable difficulties he would encounter.

Embracing Discomfort:
Running through deserts, rainforests, and high-altitude regions would test even the most seasoned endurance athletes. Cook adopted a mindset of embracing discomfort rather than resisting it. He understood that pain and fatigue were inevitable parts of the journey, and instead of

fearing them, he trained himself to accept these challenges and push through them. His previous experiences, such as running from Istanbul to London, helped him develop a strong mental fortitude that would serve him well throughout the Africa run.

5. Recovery and Injury Management
Proper recovery was essential in ensuring Cook could continue running day after day without succumbing to injury or fatigue. His recovery process was as important as his training itself.
Rest and Sleep:
Adequate sleep was crucial for muscle recovery, energy restoration, and mental clarity. Cook prioritized getting enough sleep each night, as this was when his body could repair the wear and tear caused by daily long-distance running. Sleep was also essential for maintaining his mental focus, ensuring that he could face the next day's challenges with a clear and focused mind.
Massage and Physical Therapy:
To prevent injuries and manage muscle soreness, Cook incorporated regular massages and physical therapy sessions into his routine. Deep tissue massages helped alleviate tightness and muscle strain, while physical therapy addressed any early signs of injury before they could develop into serious problems.
Cold and Heat Therapy:
Cook also used cold therapy, such as ice baths, to reduce inflammation and muscle soreness after

particularly grueling runs. Heat therapy, such as hot baths or sauna sessions, helped increase blood flow to tired muscles and speed up recovery.

Setting Off: Cape Agulhas, South Africa

On April 22, 2023, Russ Cook stood at Cape Agulhas, South Africa's southernmost point, with the vast African continent stretching out ahead of him. This marked the beginning of one of the most audacious challenges ever undertaken: to run the entire length of Africa, from Cape Agulhas to Ras Ben Sakka, Tunisia, at the northernmost tip of the continent. The sheer scale of the journey ahead—over 10,000 miles across 16 countries—was enough to daunt even the most seasoned adventurer, but for Cook, it was the culmination of years of preparation, personal reflection, and a desire to push human limits.

The Significance of Cape Agulhas
Cape Agulhas is not only the geographic starting point of Africa's southern end, but it also represents a symbolic launching pad for explorers and adventurers. It is where the Atlantic and Indian Oceans meet, creating a unique and often turbulent environment. For Cook, standing at Cape Agulhas marked both a physical and emotional milestone. As he prepared to take his first steps, the enormity of the task ahead became real. He was not only embarking on a journey through diverse

landscapes, cultures, and climates but also facing the psychological and physical challenges that come with running an average of 29 miles every day for nearly a year.

The moment was both monumental and intimate. Cook's sense of determination was visible, but so was the weight of the task ahead. As he looked north toward Tunisia, the next 352 days of his life would be shaped by this journey, and the goal was clear: to reach the northern tip of the continent using nothing but his own two feet.

The First Few Miles: A Mix of Excitement and Reality

The first day of the journey set the tone for what was to come. Cook's first run, covering a distance of 50.6 kilometers (31 miles), was both exhilarating and daunting. After months of intense training and years of dreaming about this challenge, he was finally living it. The adrenaline coursing through his veins helped him get through that first run, but even on day one, Cook was acutely aware that the road ahead would only get tougher.

In a post on Instagram after his first run, Cook acknowledged the intensity of the challenge: "Tougher days are yet to come of course, and they will be the toughest I've ever faced, no doubt. I'm ready to attack them all." His excitement was palpable, but so was his understanding of the physical and mental hurdles he would face in the coming months. Cape Agulhas offered him a smooth start, but soon, Cook would begin to feel the weight of daily ultra-distance running compounded by Africa's unpredictable terrain and weather.

The South African coastline greeted him with open arms—cool coastal breezes, relatively flat roads, and a climate he had prepared for. But as he pressed on, even within the first few days, the reality of the challenge became clear. He would not only need to summon all his physical strength but also his mental resilience to push through long stretches of isolation, exhaustion, and discomfort.

Emotional Farewells and Embracing the Road Ahead
Setting off from Cape Agulhas also meant parting ways with family, friends, and a familiar life back in Worthing, England. Although Cook's support team would accompany him for parts of the journey, there were many miles he would face alone, without the comforts of home or regular human contact. The emotional challenge of such isolation was something Cook anticipated, but it remained one of the greatest tests throughout his journey.

Cook's motivation was fueled not just by a desire for personal achievement, but also by the larger mission he had undertaken: to raise awareness and funds for mental health causes and Sahrawi cultural education. As he began his first run in South Africa, these causes weighed heavily on his mind, giving him the emotional drive needed to push through the inevitable pain and fatigue that lay ahead. Every step he took brought him closer to not just physical victory, but also to making a difference in the lives of those who benefited from his charitable work.

As the South African landscape began to unfold beneath his feet, with its stunning coastal vistas and lush natural beauty, Cook was constantly reminded of the magnificence of the African continent. This beauty would serve as both a distraction and a source of inspiration throughout his journey, offering him moments of awe and wonder amidst the grueling physical toll.

Adapting to the Routine: The First Weeks on the Road

The early days of the journey were not without their challenges. Even after years of training, the transition to running marathon distances day after day required an adjustment period. Cook had to quickly adapt to the demands of daily ultramarathons—running, recovering, refueling, and repeating the process, often with little rest or downtime. His body needed to acclimatize to the rigors of continuous long-distance running, and his mind needed to find ways to stay sharp and focused.

At this stage, Cook also began to experience the physical wear and tear that would define much of the journey. Blisters, muscle soreness, and dehydration became constant companions. Despite the smooth start, the unpredictability of Africa's terrain and weather was always a looming threat. Even in the first few weeks, Cook faced fluctuating temperatures, unpredictable winds, and stretches of road that challenged his stamina.

However, Cook's mental fortitude helped him through the early period of adjustment. His experience in completing previous endurance feats, such as running from Istanbul to London, had equipped him with the mental tools to push through moments of doubt and fatigue. His training and preparation paid off as he established a routine that allowed him to find rhythm in his runs, making each day's journey a small victory in itself.

Building Momentum and Facing the Unknown

As Russ Cook settled into his journey across South Africa, momentum began to build. Each successful day of running became a testament to his preparation, determination, and the drive to continue forward. South Africa was just the beginning, and as Cook crossed its landscapes—past mountains, coastal towns, and vast plains—he remained ever mindful that the toughest challenges were yet to come. He would soon face the deserts, jungles, and highlands of the African continent, with new countries and unfamiliar environments testing his resilience at every turn.

By the time Cook left Cape Agulhas behind, he had already proven to himself that he could adapt to the demands of running the length of a continent. But with every step northward, the unknown loomed ahead, and Cook was determined to meet it head-on, running through each new day as part of his larger mission to make a lasting impact

Chapter 3: Facing the Continent's Challenges

Navigating Africa: Countries, Cities, and Landscapes

Russ Cook's journey across Africa was not just a physical test, but a deeply immersive experience in one of the most diverse and vast continents on Earth. From the coastal plains of South Africa to the windswept deserts of the Sahara, each country he crossed presented unique challenges and beauty. Cook's route took him through 16 countries, exposing him to a myriad of landscapes, cultures, and cities, each contributing to the richness and complexity of his 352-day mission to run the length of Africa.

Southern Africa: South Africa and Namibia
Cook's journey began in South Africa, where he was greeted by the breathtaking coastal scenery of Cape Agulhas. As he made his way through the country, he traversed a variety of landscapes, from the bustling urban centers of Cape Town and Johannesburg to the sprawling farmlands and savannahs. South Africa's well-paved roads offered some comfort for the early stages of his journey, but the sheer distances involved quickly began to take their toll.

One of the first major hurdles came in Namibia. Known for its vast deserts, particularly the Namib Desert, this country posed a significant challenge to Cook's endurance and mental fortitude. The Namib, one of the driest places on Earth, subjected Cook to extreme heat, dehydration, and isolation. On Day 20, he faced severe dehydration and was forced to stop, delirious, on the side of the road. The unforgiving environment tested his limits early in the challenge, but it also highlighted the stark beauty of Namibia's landscapes—endless sand dunes, rugged mountain ranges, and open skies.
Namibia was a lesson in resilience for Cook. Despite the physical hardships, he pressed on, marveling at the surreal landscapes that stretched out before him. The contrast between the challenging terrain and the serenity of the desert became a recurring theme throughout his run. Cook's ability to adapt to such extremes in climate and geography would be critical as he ventured further into Africa.

Western Africa: Angola, Democratic Republic of Congo, and Nigeria
After leaving Namibia, Cook entered Angola, a country that presented new challenges both physical and logistical. Angola's roads were often rugged, and Cook had to navigate through remote areas where support was sparse. On Day 64, he faced a harrowing experience when he and his team were confronted by two armed men who stole cameras, phones, cash, and passports. This

incident underscored the unpredictable nature of the journey and the potential dangers of running through unfamiliar and sometimes unstable regions.

The Democratic Republic of Congo (DRC) posed its own unique challenges. As Cook ventured deeper into the jungles of the DRC, the dense forests and rugged terrain slowed his progress. Communication became difficult, and at one point, he lost contact with his support team while navigating through the jungle. Fortunately, they were later reunited, but the experience highlighted the isolation and unpredictability of his chosen path. The lush, humid environment of the DRC was a stark contrast to the arid deserts of Namibia, demonstrating the incredible diversity of Africa's ecosystems.

Nigeria, one of Africa's most populous and vibrant countries, offered a different set of experiences. The energy of the cities like Lagos and Benin City was palpable, but with that energy came new challenges. Cook faced bouts of food poisoning while in Nigeria, as well as a nagging back injury that required him to seek medical attention in Benin City. Despite these setbacks, the warmth and hospitality of the Nigerian people stood out. Locals frequently joined him for sections of his run, offering encouragement and sharing stories, which provided Cook with a sense of connection amidst the grueling nature of his journey.

The Sahel and the Sahara: Senegal, Mauritania, and Algeria

As Cook moved further north into the Sahel region, the landscape began to change dramatically once again. Senegal and Mauritania marked the transition from the verdant jungles of West Africa to the arid, semi-desert regions that lead into the Sahara. In Senegal, Cook crossed the border from Guinea, reflecting on the kindness of the people he had met along the way and the deep questions the journey had stirred in him. "When I started this mission, I was hoping that throughout the course of such a long adventure maybe I would discover more answers... but honestly, I just have more questions," Cook wrote on Instagram as he moved through Senegal.

Mauritania's vast, barren landscapes offered little in terms of physical comfort, but the simplicity of the terrain brought a new kind of clarity to Cook's mission. The endless horizons of sand dunes and the isolation of the desert provided moments of reflection and solitude. This region was known for its harshness, with scorching daytime temperatures and frigid nights. Sandstorms were frequent, and Cook often wore goggles to protect himself from the abrasive winds as he crossed the Sahara Desert. Running through the Sahara became one of the most physically and mentally demanding parts of his journey, but it also showcased the immense scale and beauty of Africa's most iconic desert.

Algeria, the gateway to North Africa, was both a logistical and physical challenge. Visa issues almost derailed the mission as Cook tried to enter the country, and the harsh desert conditions continued to test his endurance. Algeria's portion of the Sahara is notorious for its remoteness, and Cook had to rely heavily on his support team to ensure that he stayed hydrated and safe in the extreme heat. Despite these difficulties, Cook remained focused on the finish line, knowing that Tunisia was now within reach.

North Africa: Tunisia and the Finish Line
The final leg of Cook's journey took him through Tunisia, where he would complete his epic run at Ras Ben Sakka, the northernmost point of Africa. After months of traversing deserts, jungles, and savannahs, Tunisia presented a new landscape: the Mediterranean coast. As he neared the end of his journey, Cook reflected on the physical and emotional toll the past 352 days had taken on him. His body had endured countless injuries, dehydration, and exhaustion, yet his spirit remained unbroken.
On the final day of the run, as Cook approached Ras Ben Sakka, the significance of what he had accomplished began to sink in. After running more than 10,190 miles (16,400 kilometers) across some of the most challenging terrains on Earth, Cook's mission was almost complete. He was greeted by family and friends as he crossed the finish line, a moment of triumph and relief after nearly a year on the road. Cook celebrated by taking a dip in the

Mediterranean Sea, a symbolic cleansing after months of hardship and perseverance.

The Beauty of Africa: A Journey Beyond the Physical

Throughout his journey, Russ Cook consistently shared his experiences with the world through social media, documenting not only the physical challenges but also the stunning beauty of the African continent. From the towering sand dunes of the Namib Desert to the lush rainforests of the Congo, Cook witnessed firsthand the incredible diversity of Africa's landscapes. His posts highlighted the kindness and hospitality of the people he met along the way, many of whom joined him for portions of his run, offering support and encouragement.

Cook's journey through Africa was more than just a physical challenge; it was an exploration of the continent's beauty, complexity, and humanity. Each country he passed through added to the richness of the experience, from the coastal plains of South Africa to the rocky shores of Tunisia. The landscapes may have been challenging, but they were also a source of inspiration, pushing Cook to continue when the road ahead seemed impossible.

Visa Complications and Geopolitical Hurdles

Running the length of Africa was not just an endurance challenge for Russ Cook, but also a logistical and diplomatic marathon. The ultra-runner, who traversed over 16 countries on his epic journey, faced numerous visa complications and geopolitical hurdles, which threatened to derail his mission at several critical junctures. These challenges were as diverse as the terrains he crossed, ranging from visa rejections to unstable political climates, all of which added to the already demanding nature of his ultra-marathon.

Navigating Complex Visa Processes
Each African country that Cook entered required proper documentation, often with separate requirements, timelines, and procedures. Unlike a conventional traveler who might spend a few days or weeks in each country, Cook's journey took him on a prolonged path through each nation, necessitating special permits for extended stays.

One of the early challenges he faced was in acquiring visas in countries where infrastructure or diplomatic channels were not as straightforward as they might be in Europe or North America. In some cases, Cook and his team had to navigate complicated bureaucracies and overcome delays. This meant that obtaining visas in advance became crucial to maintaining momentum during the run.

Visa issues threatened to bring his mission to a halt particularly in countries like Algeria, where the entry process was fraught with delays and uncertainty. Algeria, a country Cook encountered towards the end of his journey, proved to be one of the most difficult in terms of visa negotiations. The political climate in North Africa and the heightened security concerns in the region further complicated matters, making it difficult for Cook to gain the necessary clearance. At one point, it seemed as though his ultra-marathon might end prematurely due to the delays in securing permission to cross the border. Thankfully, after much negotiation and coordination with local authorities, he was granted entry, allowing him to continue his mission.

Visa-related obstacles were a constant source of stress, as they required Cook to stay flexible with his plans and adapt his running schedule. Any delay at a border or embassy had a ripple effect, potentially pushing back his entire timeline. This added pressure to an already rigorous challenge, testing his patience and resolve just as much as his physical stamina.

Political Instability and Security Concerns
Geopolitical challenges were another significant aspect of Cook's journey. Africa, with its vast and varied political landscape, presented risks that went beyond mere logistics. Several of the countries Cook passed through were experiencing political instability, security concerns, or internal conflicts

that required careful planning and execution of his route.

One of the most dramatic incidents Cook faced was in Angola, where he and his team were victims of an armed robbery on Day 64 of the run. Two armed men approached them and stole vital equipment, including phones, cameras, cash, and even passports. This not only posed an immediate physical threat but also complicated the logistics of the journey, as the stolen passports meant that Cook's team had to engage with local authorities to recover their documentation before continuing into the next country. The robbery underscored the importance of security in regions where law enforcement and protection were limited.

In countries like the Democratic Republic of Congo (DRC), Cook faced the additional challenge of navigating through areas with limited infrastructure and potential security risks. The DRC is known for its dense jungle terrain and historical instability, both of which contributed to delays and logistical difficulties. Cook's team lost contact with him at one point while he was running through the jungle, a nerve-wracking experience that highlighted the unpredictable nature of the route.

Security concerns were ever-present, particularly in remote or politically unstable regions. Cook and his team had to be vigilant, often changing their running routes or schedules based on the latest updates from local authorities and security experts. This constant state of adaptation made the journey all the more taxing, as Cook had to remain mentally prepared for any sudden changes.

Diplomatic and Cultural Sensitivities

Navigating Africa also meant that Cook and his team had to be aware of the cultural and diplomatic nuances in each country. Africa is a continent with thousands of distinct languages, ethnic groups, and cultural traditions, making diplomacy a critical part of the journey. In some countries, Cook's team had to negotiate with local authorities, tribal leaders, or regional officials to ensure their safety and secure the necessary permissions to pass through.

There were moments when Cook's mission, which involved running through sensitive areas or national borders, required careful negotiation to avoid escalating tensions. Some of the regions Cook crossed were embroiled in long-standing political disputes or were experiencing heightened security alerts, particularly in northern Africa, where terrorism and political unrest have been ongoing concerns.

Cultural sensitivity was also crucial, as Cook moved from one country to the next. His journey brought him into contact with a wide variety of customs, languages, and local traditions, each requiring a degree of understanding and respect. Local communities often viewed his ultra-marathon with curiosity, and Cook made it a point to engage with people along the way. In some areas, locals even joined him for portions of his run, offering both moral support and logistical aid. These interactions were key in fostering goodwill and ensuring safe passage through regions that might otherwise have been more challenging to navigate.

Adapting to the Geopolitical Landscape
Cook's ultra-marathon was as much about adaptation as it was about endurance. As he made his way from southern to northern Africa, the political landscape shifted dramatically. In some countries, the roads were well-maintained and the process of crossing borders was relatively smooth. In others, particularly in parts of West Africa and the Sahel, borders were more porous, and the lack of infrastructure made it difficult to adhere to a set schedule.
One of the final hurdles came in Algeria, where Cook faced significant delays due to the strict visa requirements and the tense political situation in the region. The Sahara Desert, which Cook had to cross as part of his final push towards Tunisia, posed additional challenges not just in terms of the physical environment, but also because of the geopolitical concerns surrounding the region. Northern Africa has long been a hotspot for political unrest, and Cook's team had to carefully navigate through this area, ensuring that they stayed out of harm's way.

The Role of Technology and Support
Technology played a crucial role in helping Cook and his team manage the logistical challenges posed by visa complications and geopolitical

hurdles. Satellite phones, GPS tracking, and real-time communication with local embassies or diplomatic offices were essential tools in navigating these obstacles. Cook's support team was instrumental in coordinating with authorities across multiple countries, ensuring that he had the necessary documentation to continue his journey.

Social media also became a valuable tool in raising awareness and garnering support for the mission. By sharing his experiences on platforms like Instagram and YouTube, Cook was able to build a global following that not only motivated him but also helped in raising funds for charity. His online presence also served as a way to document the challenges he faced, including the visa issues and security concerns that arose throughout the ultra-marathon.

Overcoming Bureaucratic and Geopolitical Challenges

Russ Cook's ultra-marathon was not just a physical challenge, but also a lesson in overcoming the bureaucratic and geopolitical complexities of traversing an entire continent. The visa complications, political instability, and security concerns he faced were a testament to the unpredictable nature of such a monumental undertaking. Yet, through careful planning, adaptability, and a strong support network, Cook was able to overcome these hurdles and achieve his goal of running the length of Africa.

Cook's experience serves as a reminder of the broader challenges that come with exploring the world's most diverse and politically complex regions. His ability to navigate these geopolitical and logistical minefields, while still maintaining his focus on the mission, speaks to his resilience and determination to make a difference.

Dealing with Health Scares and Injury

Russ Cook's attempt to run the length of Africa was a monumental challenge not only in terms of endurance but also in dealing with the physical toll on his body. Over 352 days, covering over 10,190 miles, his journey was marked by numerous health scares and injuries, testing his resilience both physically and mentally. The rigors of the African climate, the unpredictable terrain, and the sheer magnitude of daily running placed tremendous stress on Cook's body, leading to dehydration, back injuries, food poisoning, and more. His ability to confront these health challenges head-on and continue his journey was a testament to his mental strength and commitment to his cause.

Severe Dehydration in the Namib Desert
One of the earliest and most severe health scares Cook faced occurred on Day 20 of his run through the Namib Desert. Known for its harsh, arid climate, the Namib Desert pushed Cook to the brink

of his physical endurance. The extreme heat and lack of shade meant that staying hydrated was a constant struggle. During this stretch, he suffered from severe dehydration, which left him delirious on the side of the road. He was forced to stop running temporarily as his body began to shut down from the lack of fluids. The incident served as a stark reminder of the life-threatening risks he faced daily.

In desert conditions like those in Namibia, the body loses water rapidly, and without proper hydration, the risk of heat exhaustion and heatstroke increases significantly. Cook's condition was so serious that it could have ended his journey prematurely. His team worked quickly to rehydrate him and ensure that he was stable enough to continue. Despite the scare, Cook pressed on, but the experience left him more cautious about monitoring his hydration levels in such extreme environments.

Back Injury in Benin City, Nigeria

As Cook continued his run, the constant pounding on his legs and back started to take its toll. One of the most persistent injuries he faced was a nagging back issue, which became particularly problematic as he made his way through Nigeria. In Benin City, he was forced to seek medical attention to get an X-ray after his back pain became too severe to ignore.

Back injuries are common among ultra-runners due to the repetitive strain placed on the spine and lower back muscles. For Cook, the pain was exacerbated by the uneven terrain and the heavy load he was carrying, which included essential supplies for the run. The X-ray revealed that the injury was not serious enough to require surgery, but it still posed a significant challenge for Cook as he continued his run. Managing the pain required regular rest, stretching, and adjustments to his running form to prevent further aggravation. Despite the discomfort, Cook was determined not to let the injury stop him from reaching his goal.

Food Poisoning and Malnutrition
Another recurring issue Cook faced during his ultra-marathon was food poisoning, which struck him multiple times as he traveled through different countries. The varying food safety standards and local diets in the regions he passed through meant that Cook was constantly at risk of gastrointestinal issues. Food poisoning can severely weaken the body, leading to dehydration, electrolyte imbalances, and fatigue — all of which are particularly dangerous for an endurance athlete.

Cook's bouts of food poisoning often left him bedridden, unable to run for several days as he recovered. These setbacks were frustrating, as they disrupted his planned schedule and put additional pressure on him to make up for lost time once he was back on his feet. Furthermore, maintaining proper nutrition during such a long and physically demanding journey was a challenge in itself. Cook needed a diet that could sustain his energy levels and provide adequate recovery, but access to the right foods was not always available. In remote areas, he had to rely on whatever food he could find, which sometimes led to further health issues.

Despite these challenges, Cook showed remarkable resilience. After each episode of illness, he would gradually build up his strength and get back on the road, determined to push through the physical toll his body was enduring.

Coping with Chronic Pain and Fatigue

Running more than a marathon a day for nearly a year naturally took a toll on Cook's body, leading to chronic pain and fatigue. The constant pounding on his joints, muscles, and bones created a cumulative effect, where even minor injuries or aches could develop into more serious issues if left untreated. As the months wore on, Cook had to battle through constant fatigue, which was exacerbated by the extreme weather conditions in many of the regions he passed through, from the blistering heat of the desert to the humidity of the rainforests.

Sleep deprivation also became a concern, as Cook often had to rise early and continue running late into the day to meet his mileage goals. The lack of proper rest, combined with the physical strain of running, left him vulnerable to injury and illness. However, Cook remained mentally strong throughout, using his determination and focus on his mission to push through the discomfort.

One of the key strategies Cook employed to manage his chronic pain was to focus on recovery during rest periods. His team helped him with massages, stretching routines, and other forms of physical therapy to alleviate the stress on his muscles and joints. He also made sure to incorporate regular rest days, which allowed his body to heal and recover, even if it meant falling behind schedule temporarily.

Mental Fortitude in the Face of Physical Breakdown
One of the most remarkable aspects of Russ Cook's journey was his ability to push through the physical challenges by drawing on his mental strength. The health scares and injuries he faced were not just physical obstacles but also psychological ones. Each time his body broke down, Cook had to find the mental resolve to keep going. This was especially true in the later stages of the run, when the cumulative effects of the months on the road began to weigh heavily on him.

Cook's motivation to raise money for charity and make a difference in the world was a driving force that kept him going, even when his body was telling him to stop. His mental toughness, honed through years of running and previous challenges, allowed him to stay focused on his end goal. He often shared his thoughts on social media, where he reflected on the difficulties he was facing but always emphasized his determination to complete the journey.

As Cook crossed each country and overcame each health scare, he demonstrated that the human body is capable of incredible feats when the mind is fully committed. His ability to manage his injuries and health challenges, while continuing to push forward, became one of the defining aspects of his journey.

Lessons Learned and Reflections
Russ Cook's experience dealing with health scares and injuries during his run across Africa highlighted the incredible resilience of the human body and mind. His journey was not just about physical endurance but also about learning to adapt to the challenges that came his way. Each health setback, whether it was dehydration, injury, or illness, was a test of his ability to persevere and find solutions to keep moving forward.

Cook's reflections on these experiences were profound. In his social media posts, he often talked about how these challenges made him stronger and more aware of his own limitations. He acknowledged that the journey had taken a toll on his body, but he also emphasized that the mental and emotional rewards of completing such an epic challenge far outweighed the physical hardships.

For Cook, the journey was not just about running — it was about pushing the boundaries of what is possible and proving that even in the face of seemingly insurmountable challenges, the human spirit can overcome.

Chapter 4: Setbacks and Survival

The Armed Robbery in Angola

One of the most harrowing moments during Russ Cook's ultramarathon across Africa occurred on Day 64, when he and his team were victims of an armed robbery in Angola. This incident not only posed a serious physical threat to Cook and his team but also highlighted the unpredictable dangers that come with attempting such an extraordinary feat across the African continent.

While navigating through Angola, a country still grappling with economic challenges and the aftermath of a long civil war, Cook and his team were approached by two armed men. The assailants, armed with guns, accosted them, making off with valuable equipment, including cameras, phones, cash, and three passports. The stolen passports were a particularly devastating blow, as they were essential for Cook's journey through multiple countries.

The robbery shook the team, not just because of the material losses but because it was a stark reminder of the risks they faced in regions where law enforcement might not be as responsive or where security could be more volatile. Despite this unsettling experience, Cook remained resilient and undeterred, a testament to his mental fortitude and commitment to completing his run across Africa.

The Immediate Impact of the Robbery

The armed robbery posed immediate logistical problems for Cook and his team. Losing cameras and phones meant that much of the documentation of his journey — a key part of his mission to raise awareness for charity and mental health — was temporarily halted. The loss of cash also affected the team's ability to cover basic expenses, such as food and transportation. However, the loss of the passports was the most pressing issue, as it created significant challenges in continuing the journey across international borders.

Navigating the complex bureaucracy of replacing stolen passports while on the road in Africa was no small feat. Cook and his team had to contact their respective embassies and begin the arduous process of applying for emergency travel documents. This involved navigating through red tape and potentially dangerous regions to visit embassy offices in larger cities. It was a significant setback that could have derailed the entire project, but Cook's determination kept him focused on finding solutions.

Russ Cook's Resilience After the Attack

Despite the trauma of the robbery, Cook remained resolute in his commitment to completing his mission. In the days following the incident, he expressed his frustration but also showed remarkable composure and resolve. In a post after the robbery, Cook reflected on the experience, saying: "One of the reasons why I wanted to run the length of Africa is because no one has ever done it before, and now we are finding out why."

Rather than being discouraged by the ordeal, Cook seemed to take it as part of the broader challenge he had set for himself. The journey, he realized, wasn't just about the physical act of running; it was about overcoming every obstacle, whether it was geographical, logistical, or even violent.

Cook's ability to process the robbery in such a constructive way speaks volumes about his mental resilience. He was fully aware of the risks involved in such a challenge, but instead of allowing fear or anger to consume him, he used the experience as fuel to continue pushing forward. His resolve to complete the run was strengthened, and he made it clear that no setback — even one as threatening as an armed robbery — would stop him from achieving his goal.

The Bigger Picture: Africa's Challenges and Beauty

The armed robbery in Angola also highlighted the complex reality of running across a continent as diverse and challenging as Africa. Throughout his journey, Cook encountered both the beauty and the difficulties of the continent. While he documented stunning landscapes and shared stories of incredible hospitality from local communities, the robbery was a reminder of the socio-economic difficulties faced by many African nations.

Angola, a country with a rich history and natural beauty, has struggled with poverty, inequality, and political instability, which can sometimes make it a dangerous place for travelers. Cook's experience in Angola was a reflection of the broader challenges faced by many in the country, as well as the risks inherent in taking on such an extreme adventure.

Despite the danger he faced, Cook also took the opportunity to reflect on the kindness he had encountered across Africa. Throughout his journey, he had been welcomed by local people who offered him food, water, and encouragement. For Cook, the robbery was an unfortunate event but not one that overshadowed the generosity and warmth he had experienced along the way.

Moving Forward After the Robbery

After dealing with the immediate fallout of the robbery, Cook and his team managed to replace their stolen passports and resume the journey. The incident did cause some delays, but Cook quickly returned to running, determined to stay on track as much as possible. His ability to bounce back from such a traumatic experience was a testament to his grit and focus.

In the weeks following the robbery, Cook continued to document his journey through Angola and beyond. He shared his experiences on social media, including the highs and lows, and emphasized that the robbery had only made him more determined to complete the run. His supporters rallied behind him, offering words of encouragement and donations to help replace the lost equipment and funds.

In the end, the armed robbery in Angola became just one more challenge for Cook to overcome on his epic journey. It didn't stop him, and in many ways, it reinforced the importance of his mission. By continuing to push forward, Cook showed that even in the face of adversity, it is possible to keep going — a message that resonated with many who followed his journey and supported his cause.

The armed robbery in Angola was one of the most dangerous and unsettling moments of Russ Cook's ultramarathon across Africa, but it also became a defining moment in his journey. His ability to remain calm, focused, and determined in the aftermath of such a traumatic event demonstrated his remarkable resilience. Cook's experience in Angola was a reminder of the unpredictable challenges that come with attempting such a monumental feat, but it also highlighted his unwavering commitment to his mission. Even in the face of armed threats, Cook refused to give up, proving that his journey was about much more than just running — it was about overcoming every obstacle in his path.

Going Missing in the Congo Jungle

One of the most intense and frightening episodes during Russ Cook's ultramarathon journey across Africa occurred when he went missing in the dense jungles of the Democratic Republic of Congo (DRC). This event tested not only his physical endurance but also his mental strength, as he faced the isolation and unpredictability of the African wilderness.

The Congo Jungle: A Daunting Challenge

The DRC is known for its vast, untamed wilderness, and the jungles of this region are some of the most challenging environments on Earth. The thick vegetation, humid climate, and remote nature of the area make navigation difficult, even for seasoned explorers. For Cook, running through this terrain added an additional layer of complexity to an already demanding challenge.

The journey through the Congo jungle was part of the western route Cook had chosen, which took him through various landscapes across the African continent. While deserts, savannahs, and urban areas all posed unique challenges, the jungle stood out due to its unpredictable nature. Wildlife, climate, and the absence of well-defined paths made this section of his journey particularly perilous.

Losing Contact with His Team

During this leg of his journey, Cook and his support team faced numerous difficulties, including the lack of reliable communication networks. As they ventured deeper into the jungle, they encountered stretches where mobile service was nonexistent, making it impossible for the team to stay in constant contact with each other.

At one point, Cook lost contact with his team completely. He had ventured ahead during one of his running sessions, and by the time his team realized they had lost track of him, it was too late to easily retrace their steps. The dense jungle, with its towering trees and thick underbrush, created a disorienting environment that made it difficult for anyone to find their way back. The fear that he might have been injured or become completely lost loomed large.

For several hours, Cook's team had no idea of his whereabouts. This was a critical moment, as the remote jungle posed significant dangers: wild animals, treacherous terrain, and the potential for severe dehydration or injury. The clock was ticking, and without proper communication, the risk of an even graver outcome became all too real.

Cook's Own Struggle

For Cook, this period of being lost in the jungle was a test of his survival instincts and mental endurance. Separated from his team and without any immediate way of calling for help, he had to rely on his knowledge of the terrain, his internal compass, and his determination to keep going.

The jungle's oppressive heat and humidity took their toll, draining his energy as he continued to run and search for signs of his team or a way out. There were moments of uncertainty, where the dense foliage and indistinguishable surroundings made it feel as though he was running in circles. The stress of being alone, combined with the physical strain of running, was immense.

Despite the overwhelming challenges, Cook remained focused on survival. He rationed his water and maintained a slow, steady pace to avoid exhaustion. In moments like these, his training and preparation were invaluable. Cook had conditioned himself to withstand long periods of physical exertion, and this stamina now served as a critical asset.

Reuniting with His Team

After hours of uncertainty and growing concern, Cook's team finally managed to reunite with him. When they found him, he was exhausted but unharmed. The relief on both sides was palpable. For the team, it was a testament to Cook's resilience and ability to push through even the most difficult of circumstances.

The reunion brought a sense of triumph, not just for overcoming the immediate danger of being lost but also for surviving one of the most difficult parts of the journey. The team quickly assessed the situation, provided Cook with much-needed food and water, and resumed their journey, thankful that this episode had not taken a darker turn.

In a post reflecting on the ordeal, Cook expressed gratitude for his safety but also acknowledged how daunting the experience had been. He recognized that while physical training was crucial, mental toughness was equally important in such situations. His ability to stay calm and focused had played a huge role in his survival.

The Broader Significance of the Congo Incident
The incident in the Congo jungle highlighted the extreme unpredictability of Cook's challenge. Running the length of Africa was not just a matter of covering vast distances; it required navigating diverse and often dangerous terrains, where the line between success and disaster was thin. It also underscored the importance of teamwork and communication in such an endeavor. While Cock was the face of the challenge, the support from his team was crucial for navigating the logistical hurdles of the journey.

This experience was a reminder that, despite all the preparation, some risks were unavoidable in such a monumental undertaking. Cook's journey across Africa was filled with obstacles, both anticipated and unforeseen. While some of these could be mitigated with careful planning, others, like getting lost in the jungle, were an inherent part of the adventure.

Coping with Dehydration, Food Poisoning, and Back Pain

Russ Cook's extraordinary journey running the length of Africa was fraught with numerous physical challenges. Among the most daunting were episodes of dehydration, bouts of food poisoning, and chronic back pain. Each of these obstacles tested his resilience and forced him to adapt his approach to the journey, ensuring that he remained on track despite the toll on his body.

Dehydration: A Constant Battle
As Cook traversed the diverse landscapes of Africa, he often encountered extreme weather conditions, particularly in regions with intense heat and arid environments. Dehydration became a significant concern, especially as he ventured through deserts and other areas with limited water sources.

During his early days in the Namib Desert, Cook faced severe dehydration that led to a critical situation. On Day 20 of his challenge, he found himself delirious on the side of the road, unable to continue running without immediate relief. The oppressive heat, combined with the physical exertion of long-distance running, took a toll on his body, leading to fatigue and a dangerous loss of fluids.

To combat dehydration, Cook had to be vigilant about his water intake. His support team worked to ensure he had access to adequate hydration. He learned to recognize the early signs of dehydration

— such as excessive thirst, dry mouth, and fatigue — and made a conscious effort to drink water regularly, even when he didn't feel thirsty.

In addition to water, Cook sometimes consumed electrolyte-rich beverages to replenish essential minerals lost through sweat. Adapting his diet and hydration strategy became crucial, especially as he moved into regions where access to clean water was limited. He also sought out natural water sources along his route and was cautious about the quality, knowing that contaminated water could lead to additional health complications.

Battling Food Poisoning

Food poisoning was another challenge that Cook had to navigate during his run. The varied culinary practices across the continent meant that he often encountered unfamiliar foods. While trying to fuel his body with the necessary nutrients, he occasionally fell victim to contaminated meals or foods that did not sit well with him.

Cook experienced several bouts of food poisoning, which left him feeling weak, nauseated, and unable to run. These episodes were particularly difficult, as they disrupted his routine and added another layer of physical strain. The gastrointestinal distress made it challenging to maintain his energy levels, as his body struggled to absorb nutrients while fighting off illness.

To cope with food poisoning, Cook learned the importance of food safety. He became more selective about where he ate, opting for reputable establishments or meals prepared by his support team when possible. He also adjusted his diet, favoring simple, easily digestible foods such as rice, bananas, and boiled potatoes during recovery periods.

When food poisoning struck, Cook focused on rehydrating and resting, allowing his body time to recover before resuming his grueling running schedule. His experience underscored the significance of nutrition in sustaining energy levels during such an arduous journey.

Chronic Back Pain: A Lingering Issue

Perhaps one of the most persistent challenges Cook faced was chronic back pain, a common ailment for long-distance runners. The repetitive strain of running on uneven terrains, coupled with carrying a backpack filled with essential gear, took a toll on his back muscles and spine. As he progressed through different countries, the discomfort became a consistent presence.

To manage his back pain, Cook relied on various strategies. He incorporated stretching and strengthening exercises into his daily routine, focusing on core stability and flexibility to alleviate pressure on his back. He understood that maintaining proper posture while running was essential, and he made a conscious effort to adjust his form whenever he felt discomfort.

In addition to physical exercises, Cook also used techniques such as foam rolling and massage to relieve tight muscles and improve blood flow. He communicated openly with his support team about his pain levels, allowing them to assist with therapeutic strategies whenever necessary.

As the challenge wore on, Cook adapted to his discomfort, finding ways to push through the pain while still being mindful of his body's limits. He recognized the importance of listening to his body, ensuring he did not push himself to the point of injury.

The Role of Mental Resilience

Through all these physical challenges—dehydration, food poisoning, and back pain—Cook demonstrated remarkable mental resilience. His journey was not merely a test of physical endurance; it required an unwavering mindset to overcome the setbacks he faced.

Cook often reflected on how these obstacles shaped his experience. He learned to embrace the discomfort and view it as part of the adventure rather than a barrier to success. Each episode of dehydration or illness served as a reminder of his vulnerability and the importance of adapting his approach to meet the challenges of the journey.

Cook's ability to cope with these physical adversities became a testament to his determination and commitment to his mission. It also highlighted the broader message of his journey: that challenges are an integral part of any significant endeavor, and overcoming them is a vital aspect of personal growth and achievement.

Russ Cook's experiences with dehydration, food poisoning, and chronic back pain illustrated the unpredictable nature of his ultramarathon across Africa. Each challenge tested his limits, forcing him to adapt his strategies and reinforce his mental resilience. In navigating these adversities, Cook not only showcased his physical capabilities but also underscored the importance of preparation, awareness, and the human spirit's ability to persevere in the face of hardship. His journey serves as an inspiring reminder that even when faced with significant obstacles, the will to continue can lead to extraordinary achievements.

Chapter 5: Pushing Through Adversity

The Power of Mental Fortitude

Russ Cook's journey running the length of Africa was as much a mental challenge as it was a physical one. Over the course of 352 days, he faced numerous adversities that tested not only his endurance but also his mental fortitude. The power of mental resilience played a crucial role in his ability to persevere through physical pain, logistical hurdles, and emotional struggles.

Embracing Adversity
From the very beginning, Cook understood that running the length of Africa would not be a smooth endeavor. Each day brought new challenges, whether it was navigating through difficult terrain, coping with extreme weather conditions, or dealing with the physical toll of long-distance running. Cook's ability to embrace these adversities set the tone for his entire journey.

Mental fortitude allowed him to see challenges as opportunities for growth rather than insurmountable obstacles. When faced with setbacks, such as the armed robbery in Angola or the dehydration crisis in the Namib Desert, he cultivated a mindset that focused on problem-solving. Instead of dwelling on the misfortunes he encountered, Cook shifted his focus to finding solutions, whether that meant altering his route, adjusting his training, or relying on his support team.

This proactive approach not only helped him navigate through tough situations but also instilled a sense of control over his circumstances. Embracing adversity empowered him to tackle the unexpected with confidence, reinforcing his determination to complete the challenge.

Developing a Strong Support System
Cook's journey was not a solitary endeavor; it involved a team of supporters, friends, and family who provided encouragement and assistance along the way. He recognized the importance of surrounding himself with positive influences, which enhanced his mental resilience. Their unwavering belief in his mission acted as a safety net, helping him cope with the inevitable lows he faced throughout the challenge.
Communication played a vital role in strengthening his support system. Cook was open about his struggles, sharing both the highs and lows of his journey through social media and personal conversations. This transparency not only fostered a sense of community but also reminded him that he was not alone in his quest. The encouragement he received from supporters worldwide, as well as the local people he encountered along the way, provided him with additional motivation to push through difficult moments.

Cultivating Mindfulness and Focus

Mental fortitude also manifested through Cook's ability to stay present and focused on his goals. Long-distance running often requires athletes to confront discomfort and fatigue; however, Cook learned to break his journey into manageable segments. By focusing on smaller milestones, he could tackle the challenge bit by bit rather than becoming overwhelmed by the enormity of running across an entire continent.

Mindfulness became an essential tool for Cook. He practiced techniques that helped him stay grounded in the moment, allowing him to appreciate the beauty of the landscapes he traversed and the people he met. This mindfulness helped mitigate feelings of anxiety and doubt, allowing him to savor each experience rather than fixating on the finish line.

When faced with physical pain or exhaustion, Cook's mental training equipped him with strategies to refocus his mind. He employed visualization techniques, imagining himself successfully completing the challenge, which reinforced his belief in his capabilities. This positive mental imagery allowed him to maintain motivation even during the toughest parts of the journey.

Overcoming Emotional Struggles

The mental toll of Cook's journey was not solely physical. Being away from family and friends for extended periods weighed heavily on him, causing emotional strain. He often expressed feelings of loneliness and longing for connection, which could have hindered his progress. However, through mental fortitude, he learned to navigate these emotional challenges.

Cook developed coping strategies to manage feelings of homesickness and stress. He prioritized regular check-ins with loved ones through video calls and social media, fostering a sense of connection even from afar. Additionally, he journaled his experiences, which served as an outlet for his emotions. Writing about his thoughts and feelings allowed him to process his journey, reflect on his growth, and reinforce his motivation.

Furthermore, Cook's commitment to mental health awareness played a significant role in shaping his mental resilience. By understanding the importance of mental well-being, he was able to advocate for himself and others, transforming his personal challenges into a broader message about the power of mental fortitude.

The Impact of Mental Fortitude on Achievement

Cook's ability to cultivate mental fortitude ultimately became the backbone of his success. Despite the numerous challenges he faced, including dehydration, illness, and injuries, his unwavering determination allowed him to push through and complete the journey. His mental strength was evident when he crossed the finish line at Ras Ben Sakka in Tunisia, where he embraced family and friends after achieving a goal that few others had attempted.

The impact of mental fortitude extended beyond the completion of the run; it served as a powerful example to others facing their own challenges. Cook's journey inspired countless individuals to confront their fears and adversities, proving that mental resilience can be as crucial as physical strength in overcoming obstacles.

Securing the Algerian Visa with Public Support

Russ Cook's journey running the length of Africa was fraught with challenges, but one of the most significant hurdles he faced was obtaining the necessary visa to cross into Algeria. This visa was crucial for him to complete his ambitious mission, and the situation surrounding it became a pivotal moment in his journey, showcasing the power of public support and social media activism.

The Visa Challenge
As Cook approached the border between Mauritania and Algeria, he encountered unexpected bureaucratic complications. Initially, he was optimistic about obtaining the visa, but as the date of his intended crossing drew closer, it became apparent that he would not receive it in time. The Algerian authorities required documentation and processing that he was unable to fulfill in the given timeframe. This setback posed

a serious threat to the completion of his journey, as he expressed in a heartfelt social media post.

The prospect of having to abandon his quest was disheartening. Cook had already invested nearly a year of his life in the challenge, overcoming numerous obstacles along the way. He was determined to find a solution but faced a situation that seemed increasingly out of his control. The uncertainty surrounding his visa made him question whether he would be able to reach the northern tip of Africa, and he openly shared these concerns with his followers.

Turning to Social Media

In an era where social media wields significant influence, Cook decided to leverage this platform to rally public support. He turned to platforms like Instagram, Twitter (now X), and YouTube, posting updates about his visa struggles and calling on his followers to help advocate for his cause. He encouraged people to reach out to the Algerian authorities on his behalf, using hashtags and public appeals to generate awareness.

Cook's appeal resonated with many of his followers, who were inspired by his determination and the audacity of his undertaking. His story was compelling, and people were eager to help him overcome this bureaucratic obstacle. The situation quickly gained traction online, leading to a surge of support from both individuals and organizations.

The Impact of Public Advocacy

The public response to Cook's situation was nothing short of remarkable. Thousands of people rallied behind him, sharing his posts and tagging the Algerian Embassy in their messages. This grassroots campaign created a sense of urgency and pressure on the authorities to act. The outpouring of support showcased the collective power of social media in influencing real-world outcomes, demonstrating how communities can come together for a common cause.

As the movement gained momentum, it captured the attention of media outlets, further amplifying his message. Stories about his journey and the visa struggle began to appear in various news reports, bringing wider awareness to his situation. The increased visibility of his challenge likely made it more difficult for the Algerian authorities to ignore the public outcry.

Securing the Visa

After days of mounting pressure and advocacy, the Algerian Embassy responded positively to the overwhelming support for Cook. They announced that they would grant him a courtesy visa "on the spot." This development was a turning point in Cook's journey, allowing him to proceed with his plans to cross into Algeria.

When he received the news, Cook expressed immense gratitude to his supporters, acknowledging that their collective efforts had made a significant difference. His determination and the unwavering support of the public had culminated in a successful resolution to the visa crisis. It was a testament to the power of community, social media, and the willingness of individuals to stand up for a cause they believed in.

The Crossing into Algeria

With the visa secured, Cook was finally able to continue his journey toward the northern tip of Africa. The crossing into Algeria marked a triumphant moment, a victory not only for him but also for everyone who had rallied behind him. It symbolized the importance of persistence, collaboration, and the impact that public support can have on overcoming seemingly insurmountable obstacles.

As he resumed his run, Cook carried with him not just the weight of his journey but also the collective spirit of those who believed in him. The experience further fueled his motivation to succeed, not only for himself but also for the causes he was supporting through his fundraising efforts. He knew that his journey represented something greater—a symbol of hope and determination that resonated with many.

Surviving the Sahara: Sandstorms and Night Runs

Russ Cook's journey running the length of Africa led him through one of the most formidable and treacherous landscapes on the continent: the

Sahara Desert. This vast expanse, known for its extreme temperatures and harsh conditions, presented significant challenges that tested both his physical endurance and mental resilience.

The Challenge of the Sahara

The Sahara Desert spans several countries, and for Cook, traversing this region involved navigating endless stretches of sand dunes, rocky plateaus, and parched terrain. The sheer scale of the desert was daunting, but Cook had prepared himself mentally for the grueling task ahead. However, nothing could have fully prepared him for the realities he faced during his crossing.

One of the most immediate challenges was the weather. The Sahara experiences drastic temperature fluctuations, with scorching heat during the day and frigid temperatures at night. Running under the intense sun posed a risk of dehydration and heat-related illnesses. Cook had to manage his hydration meticulously, ensuring he consumed enough water to sustain him through long runs while avoiding the effects of the unforgiving heat.

Battling Sandstorms

As if the extreme temperatures weren't enough, Cook also had to contend with frequent sandstorms that swept across the desert. These storms, characterized by strong winds and blowing sand, can appear suddenly, obscuring visibility and making it nearly impossible to run safely. During these episodes, Cook would find himself struggling to keep his footing, often forced to halt his progress and seek temporary shelter.

When caught in a sandstorm, the gritty sand would whip against his skin, creating a painful and disorienting experience. Cook described these moments as testing his mental fortitude, as he had to fight through not only physical discomfort but also the psychological toll of feeling vulnerable in such an isolated environment.

To prepare for these unpredictable storms, Cook adopted specific strategies, such as wearing protective gear, including goggles and masks, to shield his eyes and respiratory system from the abrasive sand. He also adjusted his running schedule, opting for early morning and late evening runs when temperatures were cooler, and the risk of storms was somewhat reduced.

Night Runs: Embracing the Darkness

Running at night became a necessity for Cook as he made his way through the Sahara. The desert's extreme daytime heat compelled him to adapt his routine, and nighttime offered a more favorable environment for running. However, night runs presented their own unique challenges.

Navigating through the desert under a blanket of stars required acute awareness and caution. With limited visibility, Cook had to rely on his headlamp to illuminate the path ahead while remaining vigilant for potential hazards such as uneven terrain or lurking wildlife. The darkness of the desert could be intimidating, amplifying feelings of solitude and vulnerability, but it also provided moments of tranquility.

Cook often found solace in the serene beauty of the Sahara at night, where the stars shone brightly against the vast expanse of darkness. He embraced the peacefulness of the night runs, using them as a time for reflection and mental clarity. These moments allowed him to connect with the vastness of the landscape while reaffirming his commitment to his goal.

Mental Resilience and Adaptation
The combination of sandstorms and night runs highlighted the necessity of mental resilience in Cook's journey. Each challenge tested his limits, but he learned to adapt and push through the discomfort. He adopted a mindset focused on perseverance, breaking his run into manageable segments, and celebrating small victories along the way.

Cook also utilized techniques such as visualization and positive affirmations to combat moments of doubt and fatigue. By envisioning the finish line and recalling the purpose behind his run, he found motivation to keep moving forward despite the hardships.

His experiences in the Sahara served as a reminder of the unpredictability of nature and the importance of preparation. Through meticulous planning, adaptability, and a strong mental focus,

Cook was able to navigate one of the most challenging phases of his journey successfully.

Chapter 6: Completing the Mission

The Final Push: Running Through Tunisia

As Russ Cook approached the culmination of his monumental journey running the length of Africa, the final stretch through Tunisia marked a poignant chapter in his odyssey. After enduring over 350 days of grueling physical challenges and emotional upheaval, Cook was determined to complete the last leg of his extraordinary quest, which would cement his legacy as the first person to run the full length of the African continent.

The Journey to Tunisia
Cook's journey began at Cape Agulhas in South Africa and took him across diverse landscapes, cultures, and countries. After overcoming significant challenges, including health scares, visa complications, armed robbery, and the harsh conditions of the Sahara Desert, he found himself in Tunisia, standing at the threshold of his final goal. The physical toll of the journey was palpable; he had run over 16,000 kilometers and completed the equivalent of 385 marathons. Despite this, Cook's spirit remained unbroken, fueled by the prospect of finishing what he had started.

Emotions on the Final Day

As Cook began his final day of running, he was accompanied by a surge of emotions. The culmination of nearly a year of relentless effort and determination brought tears to his eyes as he reflected on the journey that had transformed him. The support from friends, family, and hundreds of enthusiastic supporters who joined him in this last push provided a sense of solidarity and encouragement. Cook understood that this final stretch was not just about crossing the finish line; it was a celebration of every hardship he had overcome along the way.

On that momentous day, Cook shared with the media his thoughts as he embarked on the last 40 kilometers of his epic challenge. "One more day, one final push to get this thing done," he stated, brimming with determination. Although fatigue and pain coursed through his body, Cook's resolve was unwavering. The culmination of his journey had drawn near, and he was eager to experience the joy of accomplishment.

The Route Through Tunisia

Running through Tunisia, Cook encountered a mix of stunning landscapes, from coastal views to the rugged interior of the country. Each kilometer was a reminder of how far he had come and how much he had endured. The terrain varied, presenting its own set of challenges, but Cook was well-prepared. His experience from previous runs in different regions of Africa had equipped him with the skills to adapt to changing environments.

The final leg also brought Cook face-to-face with the vibrant culture of Tunisia. The support from local communities was evident as he passed through towns and villages, with residents cheering him on, offering encouragement, and sometimes even joining him for short stretches of the run. The warm hospitality of the Tunisian people added a sense of camaraderie to the experience, reminding Cook that he was not alone in his endeavor.

Crossing the Finish Line

After a long day filled with mixed emotions of joy, pain, and anticipation, Cook finally reached his destination: Ras Ben Sakka, the northernmost point of Africa. The moment he crossed the finish line was monumental, marking not just the end of a physical journey but the completion of a profound personal quest. Embracing his family and friends, the outpouring of emotions was palpable. The tears he had previously shed turned into tears of joy, relief, and triumph.

"I did it! I'm here!" he exclaimed as he took in the significance of his accomplishment. The Mediterranean Sea glimmered in the background, a beautiful contrast to the arduous journey he had just completed. Cook took a moment to reflect, not only on the challenges he had faced but also on the lives he had touched through his fundraising efforts for mental health charities.

A Legacy of Inspiration

Cook's final push through Tunisia and the culmination of his journey across Africa became a symbol of resilience, determination, and the power of the human spirit. He had not only run through diverse terrains and faced numerous obstacles but also raised significant funds for two charities aimed at improving the lives of young people facing challenges.

In the aftermath of his monumental journey, Cook's story became a source of inspiration for many. He exemplified how perseverance in the face of adversity could lead to extraordinary achievements. His determination to raise awareness for mental health and support charitable causes resonated with many, cementing his legacy as more than just an ultramarathon runner; he became a beacon of hope for those striving to overcome their own struggles.

Reaching Ras Ben Sakka: The Finish Line

On the 22nd of April 2024, after nearly a year of relentless effort and unyielding determination, Russ Cook finally arrived at Ras Ben Sakka, the northernmost point of Africa, marking the triumphant end of his extraordinary journey running the length of the continent. This monumental achievement not only fulfilled his ambitious goal of becoming the first person to accomplish such a feat but also stood as a testament to the power of resilience and the human spirit.

The Moment of Triumph

As Cook approached the finish line, the atmosphere was electric with anticipation and excitement. A throng of supporters, friends, and family gathered at Ras Ben Sakka to witness this historic moment. The culmination of 16,400 kilometers of running, over 350 days of hardship, and numerous challenges coalesced into a single, euphoric instant. For Cook, crossing that finish line was not just the conclusion of an arduous physical challenge; it symbolized a journey of self-discovery, healing, and profound growth.

With each step he took toward the finish line, memories of the hurdles he had overcome flooded his mind: the health scares, the violent robbery in Angola, the extreme dehydration, and even the terrifying days spent lost in the jungles of the Democratic Republic of Congo. All these experiences added weight to this moment, transforming it into a powerful testament to human resilience.

Embracing Victory

Upon crossing the finish line, Cook was met with a wave of emotion. Tears streamed down his face as he embraced his family and friends who had been there to support him throughout his journey. The love and camaraderie shared in that moment served as a powerful reminder of the bonds formed during his adventure. The cheers of the crowd resonated in his heart, and for a brief moment, the world around him faded away.

"I did it! I'm here!" he exclaimed, a mix of disbelief and elation in his voice. The enormity of his accomplishment began to sink in, accompanied by an overwhelming sense of relief and gratitude. In that instant, he was not just a runner; he was a symbol of perseverance for countless individuals who face their own struggles.

The Significance of Ras Ben Sakka

Ras Ben Sakka, with its stunning views of the Mediterranean Sea, served as a fitting backdrop for this historic moment. The location, often regarded as the edge of the African continent, represented the culmination of Cook's journey. Here, where land meets sea, Cook could finally pause to reflect on his experience.

His adventure had taken him through some of Africa's most breathtaking landscapes, from the expansive deserts of Namibia to the dense jungles of the Congo, and each step had brought him closer to understanding not just the continent but himself. The challenges he faced—be it physical pain, cultural barriers, or the mental strain of isolation—shaped him into a more resilient individual.

Celebrating the Achievement

After soaking in the moment, Cook joined his supporters in a small celebration by the sea.

Friends, family, and even local residents gathered to honor his accomplishment. Cook, always keen on spreading joy and positivity, shared stories of his journey, emphasizing the kindness he had encountered from people across Africa.
He took the time to express gratitude to those who supported him along the way, especially those who had donated to his fundraising efforts for The Running Charity and Sandblast. His campaign aimed not only to raise funds but also to shed light on mental health issues and the importance of supporting those in need. The financial goal he had set—raising £568,000—was not only achieved but surpassed, with contributions totaling over £690,000, a testament to the impact of his journey.

Reflecting on the Journey
As he took a dip in the refreshing waters of the Mediterranean, Cook was filled with a sense of closure and accomplishment. The ocean waves washed over him, symbolizing both the end of one chapter and the beginning of another. The physical and emotional toll of the journey was immense, but the lessons learned and the people met along the way would stay with him forever.
In interviews shortly after reaching Ras Ben Sakka, Cook spoke about how this journey had transformed his life. He realized that while the physical challenge was significant, the mental and emotional challenges were equally impactful. The entire experience had deepened his appreciation for the human connections forged throughout the

run and reinforced his commitment to using his story to inspire others.

Legacy of Inspiration
Russ Cook's remarkable achievement at Ras Ben Sakka resonates beyond the boundaries of his journey. It serves as a powerful reminder that with determination and support, even the most formidable challenges can be overcome. His story has become a beacon of hope, inspiring individuals facing their own battles to push through and strive for their dreams.

As he stood at the edge of Africa, looking out at the horizon, Cook understood that his journey was more than just a physical accomplishment; it was a journey of the heart, a testament to the strength of the human spirit, and an invitation for others to pursue their own adventures—wherever they may lead.

Celebrations, Supporters, and Reflections

Following the monumental achievement of running the length of Africa and reaching Ras Ben Sakka, Russ Cook entered a new phase marked by celebration, gratitude, and profound reflection. This moment was not just a personal victory; it was a collective triumph shared with supporters who had rallied behind him throughout his incredible journey.

The Celebration
The atmosphere at Ras Ben Sakka was electric with excitement. After the emotional crossing of the finish line, a celebratory gathering took shape, bringing together friends, family, and local supporters. The joy was palpable as laughter, cheers, and shouts of encouragement echoed across the coastal landscape. To commemorate this historic occasion, a small ceremony was organized, where Cook's supporters presented him with tokens of appreciation—handcrafted items representing the various cultures he had encountered during his journey.

In the spirit of celebration, the event featured local music and dance, showcasing the rich cultural heritage of Tunisia. As the sun began to set over the Mediterranean, the warmth of the gathering filled the air, allowing everyone to momentarily forget the hardships faced along the way. Cook, known for his engaging personality, took center stage, sharing light-hearted anecdotes from his travels and thanking everyone who had played a part in his journey.

Acknowledging Supporters
For Russ Cook, the support he received during his epic run was invaluable. From the very beginning, he had emphasized the importance of community and connection. Whether it was friends and family who encouraged him from afar or locals who joined

him for stretches of his run, each individual contributed to the tapestry of his experience.

In particular, Cook acknowledged his team, who faced the challenges of navigating the route, managing logistics, and providing moral support. He also highlighted the kindness of strangers, from villagers offering food and shelter to fellow runners who shared in his passion for adventure. Their unwavering support transformed his grueling journey into a shared experience, reminding him that he was never truly alone.

At the celebration, Cook expressed heartfelt gratitude for the donations that flooded in during his run, noting that the funds would make a significant impact on the charities he championed: The Running Charity and Sandblast. His commitment to raising awareness for mental health and supporting vulnerable communities resonated deeply with his supporters, creating a sense of unity among them.

Reflections on the Journey

As the festivities continued, Cook took a moment for personal reflection. Sitting by the beach, gazing at the horizon where the ocean met the sky, he considered the transformative nature of his journey. Each step he took across Africa had been a step toward personal growth, healing, and understanding. The challenges he faced—be it physical pain, emotional turmoil, or navigating complex geopolitical landscapes—had reshaped his outlook on life.

In interviews following the celebration, Cook shared how the experience forced him to confront his own limitations and fears. He realized that while the physical aspect of running was vital, the mental fortitude required to persevere through adversity was even more crucial. He spoke candidly about the loneliness he sometimes felt during long stretches of the run, emphasizing how those moments pushed him to connect with the people he met along the way.

Cook also reflected on the broader significance of his journey. He noted that running through diverse cultures and landscapes had deepened his appreciation for the interconnectedness of humanity. He had witnessed acts of kindness that transcended borders, reinforcing his belief in the goodness of people. These experiences had fueled his desire to continue making a difference, both through his future endeavors and by sharing the stories of those he encountered.

Looking Ahead

With his epic journey completed, Russ Cook found himself at a crossroads. The triumph at Ras Ben Sakka marked not only the end of a remarkable chapter but also the beginning of new opportunities. Inspired by the connections he had made and the stories he had collected, he contemplated future projects aimed at raising awareness about mental health and community support.

Cook's journey had opened his eyes to the realities faced by many individuals around the world, and he felt a renewed sense of responsibility to be a voice for those struggling with their own challenges. He expressed a desire to engage in public speaking and advocacy work, using his platform to promote the importance of mental health and the power of resilience.

As he moved forward, Cook remained committed to his mission of making a difference. The celebrations at Ras Ben Sakka, filled with joy and reflection, served as a powerful reminder that every journey—no matter how difficult—can lead to profound growth and meaningful change. Through his experiences, he hoped to inspire others to pursue their dreams, confront their fears, and recognize the power of community in overcoming life's challenges.

Chapter 7: What's Next for the Hardest Geezer?

Teasing Future Challenges: Pole to Pole

With the monumental achievement of completing his ultra-marathon across Africa, Russ Cook has not only cemented his legacy as a pioneer in endurance running but also sparked excitement for what lies ahead. As he basked in the glory of reaching Ras Ben Sakka, whispers of future adventures began to emerge, most notably his ambitious vision of a "Pole to Pole" journey. This proposed challenge aims to run from the North Pole to the South Pole, further pushing the boundaries of human endurance and exploration.

The Inspiration Behind "Pole to Pole"
The idea of a Pole to Pole run is more than just a daunting physical feat; it is rooted in a deep desire to explore the extremes of the planet while raising awareness for important global issues. For Cook, the inspiration stems from a blend of personal ambition, a love for adventure, and the potential to bring attention to pressing matters such as climate change and environmental conservation. The vast and varying landscapes that lie between the poles represent not just geographical extremes but also the beauty and fragility of our planet.

During interviews following his African journey, Cook expressed a profound appreciation for the diverse environments he encountered, from arid deserts to lush rainforests. This newfound respect for nature fueled his passion for taking on challenges that would allow him to experience and document the natural wonders of the world while advocating for their protection.

Planning for the Journey
The logistics of a Pole to Pole run are staggering. The sheer distance—approximately 13,000 kilometers (about 8,000 miles)—and the diverse climates and terrains pose significant challenges. Cook understands that planning is crucial for such a grand endeavor. Drawing from his experience in Africa, he emphasizes the importance of meticulous preparation, including securing necessary permits, ensuring proper gear for extreme weather conditions, and forming a reliable support team.

Cook also recognizes that this challenge will require a different level of physical and mental preparation. The extreme temperatures at both poles will necessitate tailored training regimens to build endurance and resilience in harsh conditions. He has already begun testing gear and equipment suited for cold-weather running, indicating that he is taking the prospect seriously.

The Role of Community and Support
Just as in his African journey, Cook acknowledges that community support will be integral to the

success of the Pole to Pole challenge. He plans to engage with various organizations focused on environmental issues, seeking partnerships that can help amplify the message of conservation. His goal is to not only complete the run but to create a platform for discussions around climate change, biodiversity, and sustainability.

Cook's past experiences have shown him the power of social media in rallying support, and he envisions using these platforms to keep followers updated on his progress, share stories from the journey, and highlight the communities he encounters along the way. By doing so, he hopes to inspire others to get involved in the movement for environmental stewardship.

The Emotional and Mental Aspect
Russ Cook's journey through Africa taught him valuable lessons about mental resilience, and he is prepared to apply these insights to the challenges ahead. He knows that running through extreme conditions, facing isolation, and encountering unpredictable obstacles will test not only his physical limits but also his mental fortitude. Drawing from his previous experiences, he intends to develop strategies to maintain a positive mindset and cope with the psychological challenges that come with such an arduous undertaking.

Cook's commitment to mental health awareness plays a crucial role in his future plans. He aims to use his Pole to Pole journey as a platform to advocate for mental wellness, emphasizing the importance of seeking help and building resilience. By sharing his own vulnerabilities and struggles, he hopes to destigmatize conversations around mental health, encouraging others to prioritize their well-being.

Looking Forward
As Russ Cook teases his ambitious Pole to Pole challenge, excitement builds within his community of supporters and fellow adventurers. His journey from the southern tip of Africa to the northern shores of Tunisia has set a precedent for what is possible, inspiring countless individuals to pursue their own passions and challenges.

While the specifics of the Pole to Pole run are still in the planning stages, one thing is clear: Cook is not one to shy away from pushing boundaries. His thirst for adventure, coupled with a strong sense of purpose, positions him as a beacon of inspiration for others. As he contemplates the next chapter of his journey, the world eagerly awaits the next bold step he will take—ready to follow him on another extraordinary adventure that promises to explore the extremes of endurance, resilience, and the beauty of our planet.

The Impact of the Africa Run: Fundraising and Awareness

Russ Cook's epic journey running the length of Africa was not only a monumental personal achievement but also a significant catalyst for fundraising and raising awareness around important social issues. Over the course of his 352-day ultra-marathon, Cook successfully transformed his physical challenge into a powerful platform for change, generating funds for charitable organizations while bringing attention to critical societal needs.

Fundraising Success

One of the most remarkable aspects of Russ Cook's Africa run was its fundraising success. He set out with a goal to raise £568,000 ($720,000) for two key charities: The Running Charity and Sandblast Ltd. The former focuses on supporting the mental health of young people facing homelessness or complex needs through running and fitness, while the latter aims to educate people about Sahrawi culture and advocate for the rights of the Sahrawi people.

By the end of his journey, Cook had exceeded his initial fundraising target, amassing over £690,000 (approximately $872,022). This significant sum can be broken down into several contributions, including individual donations, corporate sponsorships, and public support rallied through social media platforms. The substantial funds raised will help to support the ongoing missions of these charities, providing much-needed resources for their programs.

The Running Charity utilizes the funds to offer running programs that not only promote physical fitness but also foster a sense of community and belonging among participants. These programs help individuals develop resilience and coping strategies, directly addressing mental health challenges often faced by vulnerable populations. By associating Cook's physical journey with a cause that promotes mental wellness, he effectively elevated the visibility of issues surrounding youth homelessness and mental health.

Sandblast Ltd, on the other hand, uses the funds to develop educational initiatives that share the rich culture and history of the Sahrawi people, a group often overlooked in global discourse. Through workshops, community events, and digital campaigns, the charity works to advocate for cultural awareness and social justice. Cook's journey provided a unique opportunity to highlight the plight of the Sahrawi people, integrating their narrative into his run and using his platform to amplify their voice.

Raising Awareness

Beyond fundraising, Russ Cook's Africa run was instrumental in raising awareness around several pressing issues. His journey highlighted the challenges faced by marginalized communities, particularly in Africa. By documenting his experiences on social media platforms like Instagram, Twitter (now X), and YouTube, Cook provided a real-time narrative of the diverse cultures, landscapes, and challenges he encountered along the way.

One of the key issues Cook shed light on was the mental health crisis among young people, particularly those who are homeless or facing adversity. His commitment to The Running Charity allowed him to share stories of resilience and hope, emphasizing the importance of mental health resources and the positive impact of physical activity. Through his storytelling, he encouraged conversations about mental health, helping to destigmatize the struggles many face and inspiring others to seek help and support.

Cook's encounters during his run also brought attention to geopolitical issues in the countries he traversed. From visa complications in Algeria to navigating social and economic challenges in the Democratic Republic of the Congo, his journey underscored the complexities of life in different African nations. By sharing these experiences, Cook educated his audience on the realities faced by individuals living in these regions, fostering empathy and understanding.

Moreover, the cultural exchanges and connections he forged with local communities enriched his narrative. Cook documented the kindness and hospitality of the people he met, showcasing the rich cultural diversity across the continent. By sharing these interactions, he promoted cultural awareness and appreciation, encouraging his followers to recognize the importance of celebrating differences and fostering solidarity.

The Power of Social Media

Social media played a pivotal role in amplifying the impact of Cook's Africa run. His online presence allowed him to engage with a global audience, garnering support and donations while sharing compelling stories from his journey. Regular updates, photos, and videos kept his followers invested in his adventure, creating a sense of community around his mission.

Cook leveraged hashtags and collaborations with influencers and fellow athletes to broaden his reach, effectively mobilizing a network of supporters. This collective effort not only amplified his fundraising endeavors but also reinforced the message of mental health awareness and cultural education. The community that emerged around his journey became an integral part of his narrative, illustrating the power of collective action in driving social change.

Lasting Legacy

As Russ Cook reflects on his incredible journey, the impact of his Africa run will continue to resonate beyond the finish line. The funds raised will enable The Running Charity and Sandblast Ltd to expand their outreach and impact, providing resources and support to those in need. Additionally, the awareness generated will inspire others to take action—whether through participation in charity runs, advocacy for mental health resources, or engagement with cultural education.

Cook's journey serves as a reminder of the profound connection between physical challenges and social causes. His ability to intertwine personal achievement with a commitment to making a difference demonstrates that one person's journey can inspire many and spark meaningful change in society. The echoes of his Africa run will undoubtedly motivate future adventurers to consider the greater good in their pursuits, paving the way for continued dialogue and action around critical global issues.

Printed in Great Britain
by Amazon